D1432609

Maya Lin

Amy Stone

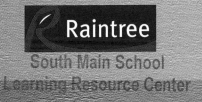

Published by Raintree, a division of Reed Elsevier, Inc.

Project Editors: Marta Segal Block, Helena Attlee
Production Manager: Brian Suderski
Designed by Ian Winton

Planned and produced by Discovery Books

Library of Congress Cataloging-in-Publication Data:

Stone, Amy, 1947-
Maya Lin / Amy Stone.
p. cm. -- (Raintree biographies)
Summary: Presents the life of the architect-sculptor who de-
signed the Vietnam War Memorial.
Includes bibliographical references and index.
ISBN 0-7398-6863-2 (HC), 1-4109-0069-X (Pbk.)
1. Lin, Maya Ying.   [1. Lin, Maya Ying. 2. Architects. 3.
Sculptors. 4. Chinese Americans--Biography. 5. Women
--Biography.]   1. Title. II. Series.
NA737.L48S76 2003
720'.92--dc21 [B]

2002154988

Printed and bound in the United States
1 2 3 4 5 6 7 8 9 0 08 07 06 05 04 03

Acknowledgments
The publishers would like to thank the following for permission to reproduce their pictures:
Corbis: 4, 5, 7, 8, 9, 11, 12, 13, 14, 15, 16, 18, 19, 20; Grand Rapids Parks and Recreation Department: 27;
The Hulton Archive: 17; Juniata College: 22; Michael Marsland / Yale University: 24, 25;
Peter Newark's Pictures: 6, 10; Rex Features: 21; Rue des Archives / BCA: cover, 22, 29;
University of Michigan: 28; The Wexner Center for the Arts, the Ohio State University;
permanent installation, commissioned by the Wexner Center for the Arts,
with support from the Wexner Center Foundation.
Photographer Richard K. Loesch: 26.

Some words are shown in bold, **like this**.
You can find out what they mean by looking in the glossary.

CONTENTS

"You've Won First Prize"

Like many college seniors, 21-year-old Maya Lin wondered about her future. "Should I go right on to graduate school," she pondered, "or find a job?" Before she could decide, something happened that she had never dreamed of: a **design** she had entered for a 1981 Vietnam War **Memorial** contest had won! Maya was about to become famous.

On June 5, 1981, a press conference was held to announce the winner of the Vietnam War Memorial contest. Maya Lin, only 21 years old, is seen here holding the model of her winning entry.

The Vietnam **Veterans'** Memorial is made up of two polished black **granite** walls set at right angles to each other. Each wall runs 245 feet (80 meters), about half the length of a soccer field. The walls rise up from the earth until they reach a height of nearly 10 feet (3 meters). The names of every U.S. citizen killed or lost in the Vietnam War are cut into the granite.

Visiting the Vietnam Veterans' Memorial often makes people feel sad. "I really did mean for people to cry," Maya said.

Maya did not know much about the Vietnam War when she created her design, since most of the fighting took place when she was a young child. At that time, the country of Vietnam was divided in two; the northern part, run by a **communist** government, was trying to take over the southern part, which was not communist.

A PRECIOUS CHILD

Maya's father, Henry Lin, came to the United States in the late 1940s, after **communists** had taken control of China. It was unsafe for Lin to stay in China because he was not a communist. A talented artist, Lin soon found work as an art professor at Ohio University, in Athens, Ohio.

Maya's mother, Julia Chang, was smuggled out of China as a child. After graduating from Smith College in 1951, Julia became a professor of English and Asian Literature at Ohio University. She soon met and then married Henry Lin.

Maya Lin's father, Henry, escaped from communist China to the U.S.. As a noncommunist, his life was in danger. This picture shows Communist Party members celebrating the new communist government in Shanghai in 1951.

The Lins' first child, a boy named Tan, was born in 1956. Today, he is a poet and Columbia University professor. Maya was born on October 5, 1959. Her middle name, Ying, means "precious stone."

Maya describes Athens, Ohio, as a perfect place to grow up. She loved to play in the woods and hills that surrounded her home.

This picture of Smith College in North Hampton, Massachusetts was taken in 1948, when Maya Lin's mother was a student there.

Childhood Games

Young Maya liked doing homework. She rarely watched television. Instead she read fantasies such as *The Hobbit* by J.R.R. Tolkien. For fun she created make-believe villages out of cardboard and pieces of ceramic.

A Top-notch Student

Maya earned good grades in high school and liked math best of all. She also enjoyed taking photos and making jewelry. Long walks in the woods led to Maya's lifelong love of nature. Maya was very serious and quiet and had few friends in high school. In college, she hoped to find more serious students like herself.

In 1977 Maya entered Yale University, one of the best colleges in the United States. She loved it there and soon made friends.

Maya was much happier at Yale University than she had been in high school.

Some people fear graveyards, but Maya did not. She liked learning how **monuments** and words could be used to honor the dead. After spending her junior year in Denmark, Maya traveled throughout Europe. She noticed that many graveyards contained trees and flowers, making them more welcoming for visitors.

In this graveyard, trees and flowers mix with the gravestones, creating a pretty and peaceful place.

Maybe it was because she did well in both math and art that Maya studied **architecture** and **sculpture** in college. **Architects** use math and drawing skills to design buildings and homes. Sculptors **design** and make statues, **memorials**, and other art works, using many different materials.

A BLACK MEMORIAL

In 1981 Maya and four other students decided to enter the contest to **design** a Vietnam **Veterans' Memorial**. They knew that the memorial would stand in Washington, D.C., between the Washington Memorial and the Lincoln Memorial. Lin and the other students decided to visit the site before starting work on their designs.

*The Lincoln Memorial, Washington, D.C. The new Vietnam Veterans' Memorial was to stand not far from this national **monument**.*

Finding Inspiration

"The design for the Vietnam Veterans' Memorial sort of popped into my head. I wanted some sort of journey into the earth."

Maya Lin

The contest organizers had expected a white memorial, but Maya knew that it had to be black. The names of all U.S. citizens killed or lost in the war would be on the memorial. Maya understood that they would show up more clearly against black **granite** than against white stone. The polished black granite would also reflect the trees, the sky, and even the visitors. Like the graveyards in Europe with their lovely gardens, Maya's memorial would bring the living and the dead together.

Unusual Methods

Before using pastel crayons to draw her Vietnam Veterans' Memorial design, Maya made a model out of mashed potatoes!

There are 58,000 names carved into the black granite of the memorial.

THE STRUGGLE BEGINS

When Maya **designed** the Vietnam **Veterans' Memorial**, she knew little about the history of the war. But she did know its cost: the people who had died. Maya believed that the memorial should honor them.

When the Vietnam War ended in 1973, nearly 58,000 Americans had been killed and 300,000 had been wounded. It was some of the surviving veterans who decided that a memorial should be built for those who had died.

Maya's ideas matched those of the contest's organizers. They were soldiers who had fought in the war and started the Vietnam Veterans' Memorial Fund. The fund was set up to raise money for a **monument** that would help Americans remember and respect the soldiers who had died.

A Lack of Confidence

Maya did not believe her Vietnam Veterans' Memorial design would win. *"It was too different, too strange,"* she said.

Not everyone was convinced that the Vietnam War was a good thing. There were many anti-Vietnam War demonstrations, like this one that took place in New York City's Central Park on April 15, 1967.

The contest judges said Maya had designed a beautiful place, "…where the simple setting of earth, sky, and remembered names" came together. Not everyone agreed. One person even described Maya's design as a "black gash of shame."

Saying Something New

Maya felt that many people did not yet understand that a memorial could differ from a statue. *"Art is and should be,"* she later said, *"the act of an individual willing to say something new…"*

THE COMPROMISE

At first, Jan Scruggs, the head of the Vietnam **Veterans' Memorial** Fund (VVMF), thought Maya's **design** looked like a bat. Before long, he came to like its simple beauty.

Jan Scruggs was the first person to pursue the idea of building a memorial for Vietnam veterans, and he became one of Maya Lin's strongest supporters.

In 1981 newspapers and magazines published articles for and against Maya's design. Some people even said that a person of Asian **descent** should not be allowed to design an American **monument**.

A Change of Heart

"Maya **epitomizes** everything that is good about this country. She was treated very poorly and I am sorry about that."

Jan Scruggs, founder of VVMF

"Go ahead with the wall," the critics said, "but add a statue of Vietnam War soldiers and an American flag." The U.S. Senate held a hearing in 1981 to discuss the memorial. Even though her voice shook a bit, Maya bravely faced the audience and the television cameras. She spoke out against the statue and flag.

In the end, *The Three Servicemen Statue*, designed by Frederick Hart, was placed at the site, well away from Lin's wall. A flag was placed at the entrance to the memorial grounds.

President Ronald Reagan holding a replica of **The Three Servicemen Statue** *during its dedication ceremony, November 1984.*

Drawing the Crowds

The wall is the most popular memorial in the United States. More than one million people visit it each year.

BUILDING THE WALL

Although the government decided that the **memorial** could be built, Maya still had a fight on her hands. The **architects** hired to build the wall sometimes behaved as though her **opinion** did not count.

Maya was sure that the names on the wall should be arranged under the dates that the soldiers died. Other people wanted them arranged in alphabetical order. Maya worried that the relatives of someone with a common name, like Charles Smith, might feel sad if they could not tell the difference between their son or brother and another Charles Smith.

Friends and family of soldiers who fought and died in the Vietnam War can come and make tracings of their names from the wall.

Crowds gathered to watch the dedication ceremony of the Vietnam Veterans' Memorial on Veterans' Day, 1982.

By **Veterans**' Day 1982, the memorial was finished. Maya visited the wall and found the name of a friend's father. "I touched it and I cried," she said. "I was another visitor, and I was reacting to it as I had **designed** it."

After earning a master's degree in **architecture** from Yale University in 1986, Maya moved to New York City. There she worked privately and quietly, creating personal pieces of artwork and planning houses. She vowed she would never make another memorial. Within a few years, however, she received an invitation too good to refuse.

THE CIVIL RIGHTS MEMORIAL

The Southern Poverty Law Center, in Montgomery, Alabama, was founded in 1971 to protect the legal rights of poor people and **minorities**. In 1988, the Center decided that they wanted to build a **memorial** in Montgomery to honor the Civil Rights Movement.

Civil Rights Movement workers in the 1950s and 1960s protested about **injustices** against African Americans. They marched, made speeches, and fought for new laws. The injustices were many. Until 1954, African-American children were not allowed to attend school with white children. African Americans were not allowed to vote. Worst of all, members of a hate group called the Ku Klux Klan were hanging African-American men for no other reason than the color of their skin.

In 1963 Birmingham, Alabama, became the focus of a series of civil rights demonstrations. Here, police officers watch student protestors who want to end the **segregation** that prevented black and white students from studying together at West End High School, Birmingham.

A Common Name

Maya Lin's name quickly came to mind when the Southern Poverty Law Center decided to build a Civil Rights Memorial. Her phone number, however, did not. They called several "M. Lins" in New York City before reaching Maya!

Maya Lin's Vietnam War Memorial had helped the nation heal from the wounds of war. The Center hoped she could **design** a memorial that would help America heal from racial injustices.

Engraved on top of the table are the names of civil rights workers who were killed and the dates of their deaths, as well as the dates of the main events in the history of civil rights. Maya made sure that the tabletop was fairly close to the ground, so that children as well as adults can touch its surface.

Maya had to read about the Civil Rights Movement before she could design the memorial. "It scared me that I knew so little," she said. "It had not been brought to my attention in school."

"LIKE A MIGHTY STREAM"

Montgomery, Alabama, is a perfect place for a Civil Rights Memorial. In 1955, Montgomery police arrested Rosa Parks, an African-American woman who refused to give up her bus seat to a white passenger. African-American men and women in Montgomery then refused to ride the buses.

Ten years later, in 1965, civil rights leader Dr. Martin Luther King, Jr. led a march from Selma, Alabama, to Montgomery. The marchers were demanding the right for African Americans to vote.

*This is Rosa Parks sitting at the front of a city bus in Montgomery, after **segregation** on the buses had been banned by the Supreme Court in 1956.*

Maya Lin is seen here at the dedication ceremony for the Civil Rights Monument, which took place during the fall of 1989. The circular top of the Monument can be seen among the crowd below.

The Civil Rights **Monument** is made up of a 12-foot (3.5-meter) wide **granite** table and a wall. The names of civil rights workers who have been killed as well as important civil rights events are carved into the tabletop. Water rises from the center of the table and flows across it.

"We will not be satisfied until justice rolls down like waters, and righteousness like a mighty stream." This Bible passage, quoted by Dr. Martin Luther King Jr., is carved into the wall behind the table.

THE PEACE CHAPEL

Evans and John Baker started a peace studies program at Juniata College in Huntingdon, Pennsylvania, in the early 1970s. As well as this, they wanted students and college visitors to take time out of their busy days to think about peace. So in 1989 they asked Maya Lin to **design** an outdoor **sculpture** in a meadow near the college **campus**. Maya liked the Bakers. They were friends of her parents and she shared their concern for world peace. She accepted the offer.

Raising Awareness

"My work originates from a simple desire to make people aware of their surroundings."

Maya Lin

Maya at work in her own studio.

The Peace Chapel is a simple design consisting of two circles. The larger circle measures 40 feet (12 meters) across. **Granite** stones somewhat larger than stuffed living room chairs line the circle's edge. When people sit on the stones, everyone is equal. No one can sit at the head of the table! In time, tall grass will grow around the circle.

The Peace Chapel's larger circle, edged with blocks of granite, seems to invite people to sit down.

The second circle is five feet (1.5 meters) across and rests on a ridge several feet above the larger ring. Maya wanted the Chapel to look as if it grew from the earth; because she sees the earth as a source of peace.

"A Topo and a Table"

The city leaders of Charlotte, North Carolina, invited Maya to **design** an outdoor art piece in front of the city sports stadium in 1990. Maya decided that large holly bushes shaped like balls would be fun.

Moving huge bushes to the stadium entrance, planting, and then shaping them proved to be quite hard work for the men who did it. Somebody had to direct the men, and Maya took on that job as well.

Topiary is the word used to describe bushes trimmed into shapes. Charlotte residents shortened the word, and fondly call Maya's art piece "Topo."

The surface of the Yale University table is seen through a sheet of moving water.

Women's Table is engraved with names in a spiral design. The spiral is meant to suggest that the history of women at Yale has a beginning but no end.

Later in 1990, Yale University invited Maya to design an outdoor **sculpture** honoring the women of Yale. Maya created a 3-foot (1-meter) high **oval**, flat table made of sea-green **granite**. Water runs gently across the table's top. A timeline beginning with the year 1701, when Yale was founded, starts at the center of the table. It **spirals** through 1990, with room for more dates to be added. By each date, Maya **engraved** the number of women admitted to Yale. From 1701 through 1969 the number is zero.

A Monument in Honor of Women

Of all the different **monuments** on Yale University's **campus**, *Women's Table* is the first and only monument to honor women.

HONORING NATURE

Much of Maya's work reflects her desire to protect and honor nature. In 1993, Maya used 43 tons (40,000 kilograms) of recycled glass to create a three-tiered landscape called *Groundswell* at the Wexner Museum of Art at Ohio State University in Columbus, Ohio.

Groundswell was inspired by Maya's childhood memories of the mounds in Mound Builders State Memorial Park near her hometown of Athens, Ohio. Ancient Native Americans called Mound Builders had molded earth into **geometric** forms, such as circles and rectangles. The forms served as **burial grounds** and temples.

Maya loved the interesting and mysterious shapes created by the Native-American Mound Builders. Their designs were the inspiration for her landscape Groundswell.

The open-air café, Ecliptic, *at Rosa Parks Circle was completed in 2001.*

In 2001 Maya **designed** *Ecliptic* at Rosa Parks Circle, a park in downtown Grand Rapids, Michigan. A circular area at the center of the park is used as an open-air café in summer. In winter it is flooded to create an ice rink. The rink is lit from beneath the ice.

In 2002 Maya created *Winter's Garden*, a three-story, 30x60-foot (9x18-meter) glass box attached to the new American Express service center in downtown Minneapolis, Minnesota. On the outside of the box, streams of water **cascade** into a pool. When the air temperature reaches zero, the water freezes, creating ice sculptures along the glass. Olive trees and benches fill the inside of the box, where the wooden floor gently ripples.

ALL ACROSS AMERICA

In 1995 PBS showed *Maya Lin: A Strong, Clear Vision*, a film focusing on 10 years of Maya's artistic life. Maya's friends were surprised. They had no idea that film crews had been following her for nearly five years!

Completed in 1995, Wave Field at the University of Michigan in Ann Arbor, Michigan, is another example of the influence of Native-American earthworks on Maya. This sculpture has a series of rectangular mounds—each of a slightly different height and width—covered with thick grass.

Maya is a very private person. Married and the mother of two young daughters, she runs a small design studio in New York City.

In 2000 Maya thought it was time to let the public know she is more than a **designer** of **memorials**. That's why she wrote *Boundaries*, a book that describes all of her work and how she thinks of herself as an artist.

Maya says that she has "...fought very, very hard to get past being known as the **monument** maker." The many beautiful buildings, houses, parks, and **sculptures** she has created establish her as one of America's best **architects** and sculptors. All of her work conveys the important connection between people and their surroundings.

Looking to the Future

Both of Maya's memorials help Americans recover from the wounds of war and **racism**. Maya cannot help but think about a more recent wound, the destruction of the World Trade Center on September 11, 2001. She believes that all Americans shared in the tragedy and hopes that a memorial will be built that helps heal the entire nation.

TIMELINE

1959 - October 5 – Maya Lin is born in Athens, Ohio, to Henry Juan Lin and Julia Chang Lin

1977 – Graduated from high school and started at Yale University

1981 – The Vietnam Veterans' Memorial Fund announced that Maya Lin had won its Vietnam Veterans' Memorial design contest. Maya's simple, angled wall design was judged better than 1,420 other entries.

1981 – Graduated from Yale University with a Bachelor of Arts degree

1981 – Worked for an architectural firm in Washington, D.C., helping to turn her design into the final Vietnam Veterans' Memorial

1981 – Testified at U.S. Senate hearing against adding a statue and a flag to the Vietnam Veterans' Memorial site

1982 – Dedication of the Vietnam Veterans' Memorial

1983 – Began graduate school at Yale University, studying architecture and sculpture

1986 – Graduated from Yale University with a master's degree in architecture

1987 – Awarded an honorary doctor of fine arts degree from Yale University

1988 – Received Presidential Design Award for the Vietnam Veterans' Memorial

1988 – Started work on the Civil Rights Monument

1989 – Designed the Peace Chapel for Juniata College in Huntingdon, Pennsylvania.

1990 – Designed "Topo" for the Charlotte Coliseum, North Carolina

1990 – Hired by Yale University to design the Women's Table in honor of Yale University's women students

1992 – Designed the new interior space for the Museum of African Art in New York City

1993 – Created *Groundswell* at the Wexner Center for the Arts in Columbus, Ohio

1995 – Created *Wave Field* at the University of Michigan in Ann Arbor, Michigan

1996 – Received American Academy of Arts and Letters "Award in Architecture"

1999 – Designed the Langston Hughes Library for the Children's Defense Fund in Clinton, Tennessee

2001 – Designed *Ecliptic* at Rosa Parks Circle, an urban park in downtown Grand Rapids, Michigan

2002 – Completed *Winter's Garden* for American Express in Minneapolis, Minnesota

GLOSSARY

architect person who designs buildings

architecture process of designing buildings

burial ground place where dead people are buried

campus grounds of a university or college

cascade to fall or drop like a waterfall

communist member of a left-wing political party that believes in state control of property, production, and trade

compromise agreement or settlement between two people or parties

descent person's national origin

design plan for an object or building

engrave carve words or lines on a surface

epitomize stand for

geometric using straight lines and simple shapes, such as circles and squares

granite very hard rock

injustice unfairness

memorial anything that helps people remember a person or event

minority small group that is different from others

monument structure, such as a building, statue, or sculpture, serving as a memorial

opinion belief based on what seems to be true

oval shaped like a flattened circle. Eggs are oval shaped.

racism belief that a particular race or people is better than others

sculpture shape carved in wood, stone, or metal

segregation the separation of whites and blacks

spiral going round and round a circular point

topiary shape cut from living plants or trees

veteran person who has served in the armed forces, often during times of war

FURTHER READING

Lin, Maya. *Boundaries*. New York: Simon and Schuster, 2000.

Stone, Tanya Lee. *America's Top 10 National Monuments*. Farmington Hills, MI: Gale Group, 1997.

Torpie, Kate. *Our National Treasures*. New York: Mondo Publishing, 2002.

INDEX